WHY NOT?

Put Your Life Together — It Belongs to You

WHY NOT?

Put Your Life Together — It Belongs to You

A GUIDE & WORKBOOK

BY RAEANN DUNLOP

Blue Skies Publishing Group

To my kids, for their never ending motivation. Being able to see life through your eyes has been an amazing journey! May you continue to view this world and everything in it with an open mind and an open heart! Never give up on your dream and continue to find your strength in the Lord! My love to you always!!

CONTENTS

INTRODUCTION
PIECE BY PIECE

Jigsaw puzzles. Who has not tried to finish one at least once in their life? Whether it is 50 or 1,500 pieces, the challenge is always there to get everything to fit just right, knowing that in the end you will have the same masterpiece that majestically covers the front of the box.

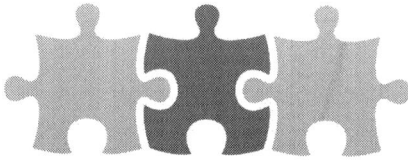

What amazes me the most is the fact that the majority of us always start with the outside border first fully knowing that the most important part of the whole puzzle is the inside. The inside pieces are what bring the picture into view. It has to be completed in order for the puzzle to come alive.

Funny how a bunch of puzzle pieces don't make any sense until you put them all together. Sounds a little bit like life, doesn't it?

Life can seem like a confusion of choices and decisions that all need to be put together in order to see the big picture. It can also seem like an endless task of going through all the wrong pieces to get the right one to fit. Life, like jigsaw puzzles, has the capability to be extremely challenging.

As you read through the following pages, I'd like you to keep this image of life as a jigsaw puzzle in mind. I'd like you to start looking at the different pieces of your life with a whole new perspective.

Ahh, jigsaw puzzles. One of the many amazing gifts that has been around for generations. Who would have ever thought that somewhere deep in the midst of cardboard and plastic film there would be a lesson in life to be shared!

Like most people, you have probably completed the frame of your life — but what are some characteristics of your personality which, like fallen puzzle pieces, have been swept under the rug? Are you living a life that someone else convinced you is the right way to live? Are you living someone else's idea of the best way to fit into society and the world around you?

Who am I?

What is our purpose? Why are we here? Why aren't we able to find and coordinate the pieces of ourselves that make us whole yet set us apart from everyone else?

Maybe one of the biggest problems is separating the things that have happened to us from the things we have made happen for ourselves.

More than likely, you have already experienced things in your life that you may regret — mistakes you wish had never happened and spontaneous choices that you feel have affected the rest of your life. Of those many choices, you, like 99% of the human population, probably handled them the way you were taught or the way someone directed you.

We all need to go through our lives in our own way to accomplish and understand why certain things and people are brought onto our path. Ultimately, it is how we react to these things and people, as well as the choices we make about them that will determine what the big picture of our lives will look like. If we don't look outside the box we will always slip into the same responses and actions.

The following pages will help you understand the normalcy of the things you have gone through, and at the same time will guide you onto a path of discovering what's important to YOU, how to make decisions for YOURSELF, and how to get the most out of the life you have left to live.

Taking Risks

Now, let's talk about those puzzles again. Have you ever walked through a toy store and stepped into the puzzle aisle? You start looking at the 100-piece and the 500-piece jigsaws, thinking it might be a little challenging but with some time you could definitely pull it off. Then your eyes get pulled into the direction of the 2,000- and 5,000-piece masterpieces — you know the kind. They're the ones only the great puzzlers can conquer. And though they are truly beautiful, you convince yourself that the smaller ones would be much easier.

After all, who wants to look like a failure for purchasing the masterpiece only to have it sit half-completed on the kitchen table? What would everyone think? "No," you tell yourself, "I'll just get the one I know I can complete that way I will feel like I accomplished something."

What you've got to remember is that we each feel and think things differently than any other person on this Earth. Not one of us is the same as another. And that simple fact means that everyone has a niche; something special that they are really good at.

Do I dare say, "Get a grip, go out and be everything you are suppose to be!" Easy for me to say, right?

I know that it's hard to venture outside of what our mind and other people tell us we can accomplish. Like the puzzle, we tend to stay within our comfort zone. Now is your time to step up and step out. Seize the moment!

Challenges

When I was young I was always pretty determined. Having two older siblings I'm sure had a lot to play into that. And although I always felt like I was different from them, there was still a part of me that knew I could do anything that they could. To have someone tell me "no" always challenged me to make it happen.

You see, from the time I was born until I was around the age of five, I had to wear leg braces periodically. Indoors, outdoors, sleeping, not sleeping, it felt like they were on my legs all the time. Those years were a very sad time in my life. It mentally and emotionally sent me on a path of insecurities and second guesses.

I remember starting kindergarten and being extremely unsure of what people would think of me and my leg braces, scared that I would have a hard time making friends. Of course, these are typical concerns of any five-year-old child, but I didn't outgrow the fear until I was a sophomore in high school. Though the braces were off, the insecurities were still there.

Every year that I got a little older it seemed like I was faced with the same frightening emotion of insecurity. Unlike kids of today, my parents didn't take me to therapy or put me on anti-depressants. I was forced to deal with my fears and had to learn to overcome them.

It's easy to see how history can play a huge part in the direction of your future. But this is where you can make the decision to stop letting the circumstances of your childhood, the things that happened to you early in your life, determine who you are. You are who you want to be. It's your choice.

I've been there. I've experienced what it feels like to be different, insecure, and afraid. I've also experienced what it feels like to be passionate about something — and have that "something" knocked out of my hands. But after many discouraging (and often unintentionally cruel) comments from people close to me, I decided to take MY life into my own hands!

What it comes down to is this; we all put our pants on one leg at a time. It doesn't matter how much money we have, who our friends and family are, or what our childhood was like. We all have what it takes to be something truly amazing.

Setbacks and Leaps of Faith

I am one of those people who, when I have an idea for something "really amazing," I tend to get really excited, really fast. Take this book, for example. This book was an amazing, life-changing idea that I got really excited about — only to have it shot down by some people in my life that didn't think it was possible. "Here she goes again," they would say. "Another big inspiration that isn't going anywhere."

I'm sure we have all faced this kind of discouragement. I'll bet that not a day passes that each and every one of us doesn't have the opportunity to do something truly amazing — and yet there is someone or something that holds us back. Whether it is someone close to us, or someone we just met, something in the world around us, or our daily circumstances, whether it is subtle or direct, those little somethings can affect how we think and what we do and detour us from pursuing something we feel deeply passionate about.

The goal of this book is to help those of you who are thinking about amazing things and grasping for someone to believe in them. I want to reach people who have an inner enthusiasm for making something great happen in their lives, but are lacking the encouragement to jump the hurdle and run.

The theory is that you can break down the wall that is holding you back from living your own life. Most importantly, this book aims to show you that the circumstances of your past don't determine who you are. In order to succeed at those two things, you will need to have the willingness to form an open mind.

I want to help you make your life happen. I want to show you how important it is to uncover your gifts and follow your dreams. I want you to know that, no matter what, you will always succeed at ANYTHING you feel passionate about. I want you to always ask the question **Why Not?** And above all, I want to see everyone and anyone live their lives as who they were born to be, not what their circumstance have formed them to be.

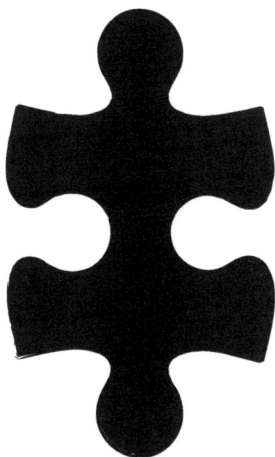

GOD GRANT ME THE SERENITY

TO ACCEPT THE THINGS I CANNOT CHANGE;

COURAGE TO CHANGE THE THINGS I CAN;

AND WISDOM TO KNOW THE DIFFERENCE.

1.
MIND OVER MATTER

I can't remember a time in my life when I didn't have the drive to do something bigger and better.

Don't get me wrong — I was never one of those kids in school that stood out, that set the trends or who was a constant leader. I wasn't a member of student council or on the cheerleading team. As a matter of fact, I was the furthest thing from outgoing you could get. I was very insecure and frequently needed a push just to open my mouth and say something.

It wasn't like I didn't want to try things; I just never had the confidence to pursue them. I lacked the motivation, self direction, and confidence needed to make anything happen on my own. By the time I reached my middle school years, I started letting circumstances determine who I was going to become.

Have you ever looked back at your past through the eyes of people who knew you or that you grew up with?

It's interesting and sometimes humorous to listen to others describe us when we were a child, or even a baby. As we listen, it can be a little overwhelming, like listening to a description of a complete stranger.

Yet, think about it: If you had to describe yourself today, it would probably be pretty similar to how others really perceive you.

{ For example, if others see you as shy or insecure, it's likely that is also how you would describe yourself. What's interesting, though, is how wrong another person's description of you — and your own identification with it — can really be. }

I firmly believe that we are all the same people we were when we were young children. That child is essentially who we are today. Sadly, it is our circumstances in life that change and redefine us. The people we are surrounded by and the situations that we endure are what shape us into who we become as adults.

Whether you are 15, 35, 50 or 80, you become wiser with each passing year. We all have experiences, accomplishments and disappointments that mark the journey of our lives. **However, if you really pay attention, you will discover that you learn something new every day.** It's an old cliché, but a strong reality.

There are so many things in our life that we don't pay much attention to. **We go through our monotonous day hour by hour, minute by minute, second by second, not thinking about the things we do over and over again.** When we actually take the time to think about the important things, it is normally not because it's something we would typically do, but because something has happened to bring it to our attention.

> **If we took the time at the end of our day to reflect on everything that had happened to us or the people that we came into contact with, there would always be something new to add to our life.**

I can't tell you how many times I have gone about my day, not thinking about anything but accomplishing the task at hand — my **To Do** list. While prioritizing my list, I am positive that I have missed many incredible opportunities due to my lack of attentiveness. Though being a list maker has its positives, ultimately it seems to focus on the stuff that, in the big scheme of things, really has little importance.

> **If you were to take 5 minutes to write down what you honestly think about on a daily basis, you would see why you lead the life that you do.**

Jot It Down

Write down some things that would be on your daily **To Do** list.

_____

_____

_____

_____

_____

_____

_____

_____

_____

_____

_____

_____

_____

_____

_____

_____

_____

_____

_____

Have you ever heard the expression **You are what you think?**

Look at your list. Does it consist of your job, things you need to accomplish at home, appointments you have to make?

If you are a parent, how far down on the list are your kids?

{ Believe it or not, less than 40% of parents in America actually spend any sort of one on one quality time with their children. }

Believe me, I get it! It's hard to get away from all the things that somehow just have to get done. On the other hand, at the end of the day, do you feel peace with what you have accomplished? Is your list consistent with the things that are truly important to you?

Jot It Down

What are two things you enjoy doing that give you a sense of accomplishment, peace, and happiness at the end of the day?

_____

_____

_____

_____

_____

_____

_____

_____

_____

_____

_____

_____

_____

_____

_____

_____

_____

_____

_____

Again, look at what you have listed. Are these things that are truly important to you? **There is a fine line between living life and just getting through it.**

Living life is doing what God has put us here to do. It is recognizing our gift and moving forward as the individuals we were born to be. The hard part is finding our gift and believing in it.

Take the first step in making it happen by **paying attention**. You'll be surprised that once you jump the fence, making changes will become a lot easier.

Words of Encouragement

The tunnel seems
long and narrow
when what is important
is waiting at the end.

Be yourself and the rest
will come naturally.

· · · *Exercises* · · ·

❶ When you were younger, what were some of things you envisioned for your future?

_____

_____

_____

_____

_____

_____

_____

_____

_____

_____

_____

_____

_____

_____

_____

_____

_____

_____

_____

_____

_____

❷ How has that vision changed?

_____

_____

_____

_____

_____

_____

_____

_____

_____

_____

_____

_____

_____

_____

_____

_____

_____

_____

_____

_____

_____

_____

Positive Reminder

ANOTHER PERSON'S POINT OF VIEW

IS WHAT IS SEEN FROM EYES THAT

ARE NOT YOU OWN.

2.
GLASS BOX

What is it that makes us so curious about other people?

Well, if it is someone we love or who we're close to, we tend to look at them for **strength, encouragement, and direction.**

We pay attention to their actions and reactions so as to get a better understanding of what it is they might be feeling. We're either protective or in some ways just plain nosy!

But when we start paying too much attention to what is happening in other people's lives, we can lose focus on what is really happening in our own. Too many times, we let another person's actions and/or reactions determine the direction, and sometimes the outcome, of our own personal situations.

Learn to distinguish the areas of your life that are in your control and the areas that are not. Take what doesn't belong to you and give it back.

Throughout my childhood I would occasionally find myself comparing certain things happening in my life to an image of a tall glass box. In this image, I would always imagine myself standing in the center of the box and everyone outside of the glass walls was looking at me, watching my every move. **Out of this impression, I created an environment for myself of insecurity and self doubt. I was always feeling that I had to live up to someone else's standards.**

During the times in my life when things were not going well I would envision arrows coming at the transparent box — some would come in and others would hit the glass and fall. It wasn't until years later that I understood the significance of these arrows and the box itself.

As I got older I started to realize that this constant, sometimes very vivid image was my mind's way of telling me that

I am original.

That as much as I wanted to be like someone else, I would always be unique. The arrows signified every choice, criticism, emotion, and mental dilemma — basically, my life circumstances.

What I didn't realize was that everyone else was original, and that they had a glass box with arrows coming at them as well.

Think of the enormous amount of pressure we put on ourselves trying to make everyone else happy. We set ourselves up for failure by thinking that we are going to let someone down that we love.

> What we forget is that the people we are so concerned about letting down have their own arrows coming at them.
>
> They are in their own glass box dealing with their own issues!

The concern, then, is allowing the problems of others to get inside our box. We get so overwhelmed with what's happening to other people that we stop paying attention to the only part that we have any control over. **Our life!**

Jot It Down

List some things going on in your life right now that are because of someone else's words or actions.

_____

_____

_____

_____

_____

_____

_____

_____

_____

_____

_____

_____

_____

_____

_____

_____

_____

_____

_____

_____

> Learn to recognize the things that are brought into your life every day.
>
> **Focus only on what is in your control.**

It's hard enough being responsible for ourselves, let alone for the choices that other people are making. To quote yet another cliché, **You have to learn to help yourself before you can help others.**

It is not an easy task; trying to focus on just **YOUR** life. However, the more time you spend looking at the hand you have been dealt, the more you will discover what you are really capable of.

Good or bad, accept one thing at a time.

Even when it is sometimes hard to understand or it seems that all that comes your way is the bad choice or the undeserving arrows. Take responsibility for your choices; put them off to the side and someday, when you really need them, the experience will become something positive for you.

Every once in awhile, spring clean your box. Throw out everything that's not yours. Give it all back to the people it belongs to. Wipe down the glass and you'll discover how much clearer the world and your part in it looks.

Words of Encouragement

You are capable of doing
AMAZING things!

The direction of your life
is determined by the choices
YOU make.

Don't let the decisions of others
pave your path.

· · · *Exercises* · · ·

❶   What are some things in your life right now that could be cleaned out of your box?

_____

_____

_____

_____

_____

_____

_____

_____

_____

_____

_____

_____

_____

_____

_____

_____

_____

_____

_____

_____

_____

❷   List a few things you could do the next time you think or feel an emotion or action coming your way that has nothing to do with you. (Meaning, there's nothing you did to cause it and nothing you can do to fix it.)

❸   Name some people in your life that have arrows in your box.

_____

_____

_____

_____

_____

_____

_____

_____

_____

_____

_____

_____

_____

_____

_____

_____

_____

_____

_____

_____

_____

_____

_____

Positive Reminder

WHEN WE START PAYING TOO MUCH

ATTENTION TO WHAT IS HAPPENING

IN OTHER PEOPLE'S LIVES,

WE TEND TO LOSE FOCUS ON WHAT

IS REALLY HAPPENING

IN OUR OWN.

3.
ROLL WITH THE PUNCHES

Discouragement and failure are two of the surest
stepping stones to success. - Dale Carnegie

There will be many times on your journey when you will doubt yourself. There will be times when you feel a power struggle between what you want and what the world seems to want for you.

Don't worry: it's normal.

> When life starts coming at you full force and you feel yourself getting knocked down, over and over again, jump to your feet! Dig your toes in deep and find the confidence to hang on!

Look, there will always be something that **comes up**, or someone who will tell you that you **can't**. These people may even come up with some pretty justifiable reasons for why your choice isn't logical or realistic.

Don't let that hold you back! You must be feeling passionate about this decision for a reason. That little voice deep inside of you is telling you that it's not impossible! **So go with it!**

Besides, what's the worst thing that could happen?

That you don't succeed?

Forget about it.

No matter what, you will always be a success because you tried to accomplish something that you feel very deeply about.

If you don't succeed that doesn't mean that you're a failure and that all your hard work just went down the drain. It just means that there is something else better out there for you to put your heart and soul into. You tried it! You're a success just for making an effort!

> **Move on to one of the other incredible things that you feel passionate about.**
>
> **Continue to ask the questions and do the research.**
>
> **Make your world happen!**

You already know what it feels like to have people discourage you so don't be surprised when it happens.

Move forward with determination and drive. You will find that with each idea you pursue, you will learn something new; something that will be used or shared on the path of your life.

Now how exciting is that?!!!

You will continue to grow and while you do, you will be encouraging other people along the way.

Jot It Down

What are some items on your list of things you want to accomplish?

_____

_____

_____

_____

_____

_____

_____

_____

_____

_____

_____

_____

_____

_____

_____

_____

_____

_____

_____

_____

_____

_____

If you look at successful people in our society, you will see that many of them have succeeded only because someone was holding them back, and not pushing them forward. Someone important in their life told them they were foolish for dreaming big. Still, they stepped up to the plate, took something they genuinely felt excited about and made it happen. Even with a lot of self doubt, they pursued their dream. There was something telling them to not give up.

Jot It Down

Name some successful people doing what it is that you want to do.

_____

_____

_____

_____

_____

_____

_____

_____

_____

Although you may have never had a world-changing idea, stay strong and believe in yourself! It's going to take some time. There is a thick shell around you that needs to be gradually chipped away. You are accustomed to thinking and living a certain way. **To break free from that is something that will require a lot of patience and faith.**

Before you know it, you will see things changing in yourself. You will start to become more **determined and confident**.

For some, this will be something new, not just to yourself but to those close to you as well.

That's the time when others will either start taking you seriously or start questioning and doubting you.

After all, that isn't you! That isn't the person they raised or grew up with!

It will take some adjusting, and of course some motivation, to show others this **new you**, this **real you** that has been tucked away for so long. The little child who didn't think twice before expressing his or her thoughts will slowly start to make their way back to the surface.

Before long, others will come to believe in this new energetic you; this person who has passion and determination for the things around them.

When I started telling people close to me that I was writing a book, deep down I was optimistic they would **ALL** be supportive and encouraging. However, I was also realistic in the fact that I knew the majority would be discouraging and negative. In the end, I was thrilled to learn that there were many who believed in me and knew what I was capable of long before I recognized it in myself. They saw the determination and confidence in me from the beginning and were waiting for it to hit the surface. That recognition and encouragement was enough to motivate and push me to move forward.

Moving forward and expressing who you really are will be an inspiration for the people close to you.

Who knows, you may even make a mark on someone you don't even know.

For those of you who don't think you are making a difference in someone else's life, believe me, your example is definitely standing out to people who are looking for some positive direction. Half the time you're not even trying. It just shines from within you.

So you see, there will always be someone or something that holds you back. The question you have to ask is,

Am I doing this for someone else, or
am I doing it for myself?

Don't ever feel like you are being selfish by pursuing something that you feel passionate about.

> **You are never selfish for going after something that makes you happy and fulfilled. It will lead you to be a better spouse, parent, daughter/son, sibling, and friend.**

Remember: **Life Happens**. Don't expect everything to be great and wonderful all the time. The reality is that people will often discourage you and doors will be shut. Take the good with the bad and keep on fighting!

Words of Encouragement

Break away from the place
of yearning for appreciation
and be who you are.

Everything else
will fall into place.

· · · *Exercises* · · ·

❶ What parts of your life feels like a power struggle between you and the things happening around you?

_____

_____

_____

_____

_____

_____

_____

_____

_____

_____

_____

_____

_____

_____

_____

_____

_____

_____

_____

_____

_____

_____

_____

_____

_____

❷   What kinds of research would you need to do or questions would you need to ask in order to move forward with at least one of the items on your Things I Want to Accomplish list?

_____

_____

_____

_____

_____

_____

_____

_____

_____

_____

_____

_____

_____

_____

_____

_____

_____

_____

_____

_____

_____

_____

_____

_____

❸   Who are some of the people in your life who could be encouraged or motivated by your newfound growth, excitement, and drive?

_____

_____

_____

_____

_____

_____

_____

_____

_____

_____

_____

_____

_____

_____

_____

_____

_____

_____

_____

_____

_____

_____

_____

Positive Reminder

YOU ARE NEVER SELFISH

FOR PURSUING SOMETHING

THAT MAKES YOU FEEL

HAPPY AND FULFILLED.

4.
RECOGNIZE YOUR STRENGTHS

Don't aim for success if you want it; just do
what you love and believe in, and it will come
naturally. - David Frost

How many of you, when asked, could list at least 3 of your strengths? How easy would it be? Would you be able to roll them off the tip of your tongue or would you have to stop and think about it?

> Many of us don't know what our strengths are, let alone have to make a list of them. We tend to see our strengths in terms of how others see us.

Take some time to write down what you feel some of your true strengths are. Once you see it in writing you will be amazed at the description of **you** others have been missing out on for so long.

Jot It Down

List up to 5 words you would use to describe who you are.
Remember it's not how others would describe you but how
You see yourself.

I am ....

I am ....

I am ....

I am ....

I am ....

Sure, there are some personal traits you have, and probably
always have had, that would be at the top of your list. These
are the things you have held onto since childhood that have
helped design who you are today.

For example, if your mother always described you as energetic, fearless, and organized, then you probably see yourself as energetic, fearless, and organized. These personality thumbtacks can be the star points to the image of your identity and sometimes, they can be extremely hard to let go of when you are trying to discover who it is you really are.

Jot It Down

What is one thing that you believe is a misperception about you?

_____

_____

_____

_____

_____

_____

_____

_____

_____

What are two things other people would be surprised to know about you?

Get in tune with who you are. Step up to the mirror and take a good look at who you see. Sort out what part of you belongs to you and what part was formed by others' opinions of you. You need to look at who you are on the inside before you can polish what you are on the outside.

Jot It Down

Look in the mirror. How would you describe the person you see?

_____

_____

_____

_____

_____

_____

_____

_____

Your own talents and strengths are the things that are God-given, not something that was taught, bought, or forced into your mind.

{ Growing up I was always so frustrated when people would try to tell me who I was. I came from a very large family in a small farm community so I was always referred to by my last name, "Vitek". I had lots of aunts and uncles and many cousins, so if someone didn't know me personally, they knew of me or one of my family members. I always felt that I had to live up to my name or be someone I wasn't just because that was what was expected of me. About the time I tried to prove my independence was the same time I was pushed back into my set of boundaries. }

A big **thank you** goes out to our parents who have given us our chemical make-up — that infamous gene pool that gives us our bright eyes and sparkling smile. There's no way to get around it. It is what it is.

However, what we own that **can** be changed **and** what makes us different from everyone else is the inner part of our mind and soul. It is that part of us that keeps us special and unique and sets us apart from everyone else in this world.

Each of us feels and thinks differently than anyone else. There is not one person out there who is exactly like you.

We all eventually come to a point where **we have to step away from our familiar environment and re-evaluate.** Knowing this, every single one of us will take our inner most passions and abilities to move forward and do something powerful and amazing with our lives.

Think about what really makes you feel fulfilled. What are some of the things you do that bring you the most joy? Write them down and just look at them for a minute. Are there items on your list that make your adrenalin sky rocket? If so, think about how time and circumstances have changed how you look at certain areas of your life.

Jot It Down

What are some things you do that bring you the most joy and, at the end of the day, give you a sense of peace of fulfillment?

_____

_____

_____

_____

_____

_____

_____

_____

_____

Look at your list and start thinking about how you can act on at least one of these items every day. Whether it be something little or something extraordinary, what can you do **today** to implement one of these incredible personality traits that makes you, you!

_____

_____

_____

_____

_____

_____

_____

_____

_____

Don't limit yourself to your surroundings, the economy, or anything else that stands in your way.

It's hard to keep the confidence when everything around you seems like it is out of control, but don't doubt yourself. The minute doubt and second guesses start setting in, the adrenalin stops flowing. You will start questioning yourself and eventually you will stop moving forward. **There is no reason that you can't excel at anything you try to accomplish.** You just need to take the initiative and find the motivation to keep going.

As I mentioned in the previous chapter, take a serious look at other people that are succeeding at doing what you love. How did they get there? If they're doing it, why can't you? **Why Not?** You could come up with a million reasons, I'm sure, but don't limit yourself. You would be surprised at the people in your community, around your state, the country, or even the world that would be willing to listen to what you have to say.

Jot It Down

What are some things you would excel at if given the opportunity?

_____

_____

_____

_____

_____

_____

_____

_____

_____

_____

_____

> DON'T GIVE UP! Continue on until you feel it in your heart and gut that it's time to stop. That strong, indescribable feeling is your mind's way of saying that you have given it 110% and it is time to move on to the next amazing thing.

Being able to recognize your abilities and gifts is a powerful thing. You will start to see that for the longest time you have been holding something back. You will begin to discover the part of you that hasn't been seen in a very long time, if ever.

Slowly you will start to break the shell that has been building up during the course of your life, and something truly magnificent will begin to be reborn!

If you focus on your strengths and gifts on a daily basis you will truly see incredible changes in your life. It will be a life filled with remarkable purpose and no regrets.

> Take action and implement a plan. Bring in positive people that can share in your journey. They will keep you grounded and focused on the end result. Whether fruitful, physical, mental, or spiritual, the outcome will be astounding!

Words of Encouragement

You are a one of a kind;
an original masterpiece.
Sign your name to the life
you have achieved.

· · · *Exercises* · · ·

❶ When you looked at your reflection in the mirror, what did you see that belonged to someone else?

❷ From the reflection list you've just made, what are some of YOUR traits that are unchanged from when you were a child?

_____

_____

_____

_____

_____

_____

_____

_____

_____

_____

_____

_____

_____

_____

_____

_____

_____

_____

_____

_____

_____

Positive Reminder

YOU NEED TO LOOK AT

WHO YOU ARE ON THE INSIDE

BEFORE YOU CAN POLISH

WHAT YOU ARE ON THE OUTSIDE.

5.
SHOW NO SHAME

Success is to be measured not so much by
the position that one has reached in life,
as by the obstacles which he has overcome.
- Booker T. Washington

Don't be ashamed of your circumstances or the results and choices that come from them. You may not like the hand you have been dealt, but it's yours.

There is intention and purpose behind why these situations have been put onto your path. It is up to you and only you to make the most out of them.

If you think back over the course of your lifetime, I am positive you will come up with a handful of times a life-changing decision has been thrown onto your path. These are the split-second choices that, if you would have decided to go the opposite way, your life would be completely different.

Jot It Down

What are some of the split-second, life-changing choices
you have made?

_____

_____

_____

_____

_____

_____

_____

_____

_____

_____

_____

_____

_____

_____

_____

_____

_____

_____

_____

> Don't reflect on these times with regret, even if the outcome was not what you had hoped for. Everything really does happen for a reason.

You can look back on these decisions and continue to wish that you would have made a different choice, **or** you can take these events and use them to make a positive impact on your life and the lives of others. Be secure in the fact that you have been given choices for a reason.

√ Take these moments as opportunities for you to make a decision — good or bad — that will lay a brick in the path to the rest of your life.

√ Take those times and think about what you want out of your life.

√ Use these choices to establish and fulfill what it is you would like to accomplish. Look at each opportunity as a choice and make every effort to not have any regrets.

√ No matter what you choose, you will make it something remarkable.

I remember a moment in my life that I had to make a split-second decision of my own. It didn't seem so altering at the time, but it moved my life in a whole new direction. I was twenty years old and was driving home to Michigan from New York, where I had been working and going to school. It was summer break and my plan was to come home for a month or two and then go back. As a matter of fact, I didn't even say goodbye to my friends and co-workers because, in my mind, I knew I would be back. You see, I was going to school to be an architect, and that summer I was making plans to do an internship in Rome.

So, I was driving through Pennsylvania on my way back home and something in my gut told me to pull over. I stopped at the nearest rest area, sat in my car, and briefly thought about what I was doing and where I was going. For one quick second, I told myself that I could still turn around and go back to New York.

I'm confident now that a part of me knew that things would never be the same; that once I returned home it would not be easy for me to return to New York. I chose to continue my voyage home convincing myself that it was temporary...just a visit. Little did I know that it would be five years before I would return. Although I am grateful now for the gifts my unplanned journey brought me, a part of me has always wondered, "what if?" Choosing not to return to New York was something I had regretted for a long time, but I eventually realized that everything I needed for that period of my life was in Michigan.

Reflect on the **positive emotion** you get when you feel strongly about something. You know what I'm talking about, that incredible sense of strength and purpose you feel in your gut. It's so powerful that when you try to define it, you can't even describe it.

We all can get that feeling every day. You will know when it comes to you. Like the many choices you have made before, this decision will somehow impact your life. **Good, bad, little or big it's all a part of your journey.**

However, what sets you apart from everyone else is that you are willing to do something about it.

Jot It Down

What are some ideas you have felt strongly about that have given you a sense of strength and purpose?

Remind yourself of the reasons you want to pursue your passions. Sometimes it takes writing your reasons down, to remember what you're in it for. Do whatever it takes. Only you know what motivates and drives you. And who knows, maybe you will encourage and inspire someone else along the way!

Words of Encouragement

Your circumstances have been
given to you for a reason.
If God didn't think you could
handle them, He would have
given them to someone else.

Open up that pocket of confidence,
stand strong and press forward.
Eventually the sand
will turn to gravel,
the gravel to cement
and walking through the storm
will seem pretty easy.
One step at a time!

· · · *Exercises* · · ·

❶ List some of the reasons why you want to pursue your passions.

_____

_____

_____

_____

_____

_____

_____

_____

_____

_____

_____

_____

_____

_____

_____

_____

_____

_____

_____

_____

_____

_____

_____

❷ Name some things that motivate you.

❸ Name some things that discourage you.

❹   How can you use some of your life altering decisions to help someone else?

_____

_____

_____

_____

_____

_____

_____

_____

_____

_____

_____

_____

_____

_____

_____

_____

_____

_____

_____

_____

_____

_____

Positive Reminder

BE PROUD OF THE STRENGTHS

YOU HAVE BEEN GIVEN.

THEY ARE THE MAIN INGREDIENTS

TO A FULL AND CONTENT LIFE.

6.
COPY CAT

That some achieve great success, is proof
to all that others can achieve it as well.
— Abraham Lincoln

Have you ever watched a baby mimic something that he or she has seen someone do? They are so serious, yet sometimes very funny and cute to watch. When trying to accomplish the task, they don't think twice about who is watching or what others are thinking. They are just naturally little copy cats.

It's amazing how much curiosity we're born with. By nature, we are so intrigued with how things work and feel. But more importantly, by the response that's received from it all. **As we become toddlers, if our actions make someone laugh, we want to continue with the act because we think it makes people happy.** On the other hand, if we are doing something that makes someone sad or mad, we stop, or at least hesitate before doing it again.

I don't think we ever really lose that curiosity until the day that someone starts telling us "no." Originally it comes from our parents, for our own safety, of course. But later on we start to hear it from others. Eventually, as we go through the stages of being a toddler to becoming an adult, we base our decisions and actions on what we have been told is right or wrong and by what we see around us.

We are influenced by so many people as we grow up — parents, siblings, close friends and others. For good reason, we find it comfortable to stay within the boundary that was designed to protect and surround us with the knowledge of what is right and wrong. To jump out of that boundary and discover new things is scary and uncomfortable because the outcome is so uncertain.

Those boundaries are what we base our decisions and our lives on as we become adults. After all, we don't know any different. All we have is what our parents believed and how they taught us. Of course, they were brought up the same way, so sometimes, it is hard to break the cycle.

It's not really until we become teenagers that we start testing our inquisitiveness on our own. **Most of us learn from our mistakes by trying the majority of things once**, only to realize how painful, hurtful, or even deadly they can be. Nevertheless, we experience it for ourselves in order to accept it as true.

Jot It Down

What are some of the painful mistakes you made when you were younger?

_____

_____

_____

_____

_____

_____

_____

_____

_____

_____

_____

_____

_____

_____

_____

_____

_____

Try to remember these early misjudgments and be open-minded about what is being said or done around you. It's so easy to judge when you don't agree with someone.

REMEMBER:

Don't criticize others because...
That would make you a hypocrite.
Don't judge others because...
That would make you God.

Jot It Down

Who are some of the people in your life that you tend to judge or criticize when they don't act or react the way you think they should?

_____

_____

_____

_____

_____

_____

_____

_____

> Everyone you meet is brought into your
> life to impact you in some way. Listen to
> what they have to say and also look at
> their actions. How they will affect your life
> and the plans that you have made?

This is also a great opportunity to reflect on how your own behavior has affected others. How many people are watching everything you do or say? Often, we are so distracted with the **important** things in our lives — paying bills, making appointments, etc. — that we don't realize our influence factor is hitting the red zone.

{ What's even more surprising is that we don't recognize when we are at the **high impact** level of that influence factor. Be aware of the fact that you are doing things on a daily basis that are truly impacting the people around you every second of the day. }

Every person you come into contact with watches how you respond or react to things, even if for just a brief second. If a situation puts a smile on your face, then others are likely to act the same way when they are faced with a similar task or challenge. After all who doesn't want some happiness in their life, right? A smile can turn around some pretty terrible things.

On the opposite side of the coin, people also look at the negative things you may be doing or saying. The **good** they will ALWAYS remember. The **bad** they will NEVER forget.

Jot It Down

What are some things you've done in the last week, in someone else's presence, that your proud of?

_____

_____

_____

_____

_____

_____

_____

_____

_____

_____

_____

_____

_____

_____

_____

_____

_____

_____

_____

_____

What are some things you've done in the last week that you are not so proud of?

Don't get this confused with what was mentioned in earlier chapters about feeling the need to please everyone else. There is a difference between **living your life for someone else** and **just living your life.** Just living your life is **YOU** being **YOU!**

> Your comfort, ease, and confidence will naturally affect the people around you. Think about how powerful that is! What extraordinary things we could do with our words and actions. It is something very empowering that can take a strong hold on who you are as a person.

People are constantly looking for positive direction. From the time we take our first breath to the time we take our last, we watch others and look for an answer to life's trials and tribulations. **We all want the good things in our lives: positive words, actions, reactions, and direction.** It's just a matter of finding what works best for us, and not for someone else.

In some cases, our reactions and choices are a reflection of someone else's decision, viewed by us at one point and time in our lives. Until, of course, we realize that we are capable of making some pretty amazing decisions just fine on our own.

Jot It Down

What are some things you do on a daily basis that are revolved around what someone else expects of you?

_____

_____

_____

_____

_____

_____

_____

_____

_____

_____

_____

_____

_____

_____

_____

_____

_____

_____

Now is your chance to break the mold. If you are reading this, it means that you are interested in cracking through that shell. Maybe you are even looking at making a difference, not in only just your life, but the lives of people around you.

It doesn't take something enormous and gigantic to make a positive impact. It can be something small and meaningful and still be very significant in the eyes of a person who is looking for direction.

Rub off on someone else. Make a positive impact and watch how it begins to get repeated, one person at a time, all because you believed in yourself and persevered.

It is an incredible feeling to have someone tell you that you have made an impact on their life. Because of something you said or did, their life has changed. It is an emotion like no other. What a great feeling to know that you have helped others make a difference. If they haven't already done so, they will eventually make a positive impact on someone else because of you.

If there is anything I could say, let it be the fact that you could possibly make a **huge impression** on another person's life.

Others will see the positive things occurring in your life and will start to look at themselves in the mirror. They will want to know what it is that makes you so happy and peaceful.

They, too, will start to discover the passion and drive inside of them that will set them apart from everyone else. Just remember that you can only control what happens in your life. Lead by example. It will be up to others to make the changes in their own lives.

> The pleasure that you get from working at your own goals is exhilarating enough. You won't have to do anything but be yourself to have it impact the people around you. The overflow of your success will influence anyone you come in contact with.

If you are one of those people that have been in **self-destruct mode** more times than you can count, think about the impact that has made on your life. How different could it be if you had looked at things in a completely different way?

The great thing is that you have been given an amazing opportunity to take what you have learned in "self-destruct mode" and turn things around. Make use of your new-found wisdom to make a difference.

Words of Encouragement

You have the power to make
some pretty amazing choices.
Keep your eyes
on the path in front of you
and look at everything
that comes your way
as an opportunity to better yourself.

· · · Exercises · · ·

❶ What are some things in others that influence you in a positive way?

_____

_____

_____

_____

_____

_____

_____

_____

_____

_____

_____

_____

_____

_____

_____

_____

_____

_____

_____

_____

_____

_____

_____

❷　What are some things in others that influence you in a negative way?

❸ Where are some of the places you go on a daily basis that you could easily influence other people?

_____

_____

_____

_____

_____

_____

_____

_____

_____

_____

_____

_____

_____

_____

_____

_____

_____

_____

_____

_____

_____

_____

Positive Reminder

OTHERS WILL SEE THE POSITIVE THINGS

THAT ARE OCCURRING IN YOUR LIFE

AND WILL START TO LOOK

AT THEMSELVES IN THE MIRROR.

7.
YOUR PERSONAL ARMY

There are high spots in all of our lives
and most of them have come about through
encouragement from someone else.
- George Matthew Adams

Moving into the next chapter of your life won't be easy and is difficult to take on by yourself — but what an incredible adventure you are on! Take this time to utilize the people around you.

Think of everyone in your life who, if given the opportunity, would jump at being a part of your new-found journey. These aren't just the **"I'll say it when you need it"** people. These are the **"I'll stop whatever I'm doing to keep you motivated and on the straight path"** people. Nine times out of ten, these individuals have always expressed how much they believe in you, you just didn't want to listen to them.

Look at it this way. **Does a general in the army fight the enemy on his own? No!** He relies on his many troops to help him fight the battle. The soldiers wait for the general's commands, and then give him whatever he needs to go into combat. Your "troops" are waiting for your command. They can't help you until they know what you need.

Jot It Down

List 3 or more people that you could count on to motivate and encourage you, no matter what.

_____

_____

_____

_____

_____

_____

_____

_____

_____

_____

_____

_____

_____

_____

_____

This falls back on what we discussed in previous chapters about paying attention to the people around you. Whether it be subtle or extremely obvious, there are people around you doing or saying things that will inspire you. These are little "**aha**" moments that were not planned, but somehow made a huge impact on the outlook of your life. These are the people that have had the "nose bleed" seats to the drama called "**Your Life**." They have been cheering you on from the beginning but have not had the benefit of sitting in the front row.

> I remember having an "aha" moment in my early twenties that involved someone pushing me to be something better. It was during a time when all I could see was the negative. The positive aspects in my life seemed very far and few between. Then, with a few words that I happened to be listening to, my eyes were opened up wide. It was like, "Hey! Wake up and enjoy the moment! Don't focus on how things DIDN'T go for you. Look at what it gave you!"
>
> I never acknowledged that person for saying something important, and to this day have never told them they changed my life. However, they did. These unplanned situations are the regular kinds of things that happen to us on a daily basis that are life-changing and monumental — but we have to be paying attention.

So each time you're with someone, ask yourself a couple of questions:

"What is it about this person or this situation that has made me a better person?"

"What can I learn from this experience/person that I can share with someone else?"

Regardless of whether it is a positive or a negative impact, it will make a difference in your life. It's not the situation that is challenging; it's how you respond to it that matters.

Every person we meet is brought into our lives for a reason. Whether it is a stranger or someone we have known our whole lives, they all have the power to change our life. It could be something they say, something they do, or the situation that we experience when with them that we will take with us forever. Therefore, don't take anyone for granted, good or bad, they will always have something to give you.

Jot It Down

Who are some of the people, in the last week, that have given you directly or indirectly, something to remember?

_____

_____

_____

_____

_____

_____

_____

_____

_____

_____

_____

_____

_____

_____

_____

_____

_____

Use these opportunities to make every task you face turn into something remarkable. Great people are given great challenges. **If you didn't have the power or strength to handle it, it would not have been given to you.**

You have what it takes to overcome any struggle and to do something incredible with what you have. In every negative there is a positive. Find what it is and amplify it. **Put the negative in the trash and put the positive in your pocket. You will need it someday.**

It is not easy! You will feel yourself taking two steps forward, only to catch yourself jumping three steps back. That's when you know it is time to bring in the troops. Pull out the megaphone and shout it loud. **"PLEASE HELP ME! I CAN'T DO THIS ALONE!"** Your **army** has your back. Take advantage of the excitement and determination they have about everything you're on your way to accomplishing.

> When I originally had the idea about writing a book, I had too much pride to ask the people around me for help. I was standing on the fence just waiting for someone to give me a push, not realizing that my "army" was waiting for me to ask for help. Whether it is a pat on the back or a shove with a metal rod, the people around you will give you what you need to succeed.

When things seem overwhelming or out of hand, call in your troops. Fill them in on what challenges you are facing and you will be surprised at the incredible advice and motivation they will give you.

Words of Encouragement

Be aware of your surroundings
and the people that come
onto your path.
Good or bad
they will contribute to
the stepping stones
towards your future.

· · · *Exercises* · · ·

❶ Looking back, what would you say a few of your "aha" moments would be?

_____

_____

_____

_____

_____

_____

_____

_____

_____

_____

_____

_____

_____

_____

_____

_____

_____

_____

_____

_____

_____

_____

❷   What are some situations where you have felt that you were making progress only to be thrown three steps back?

_____

_____

_____

_____

_____

_____

_____

_____

_____

_____

_____

_____

_____

_____

_____

_____

_____

_____

_____

_____

_____

_____

_____

Positive Reminder

WHAT AN INCREDIBLE ADVENTURE

YOU ARE ON.

MOVING INTO THE NEXT CHAPTER

OF YOUR LIFE WON'T BE EASY

AND IS DIFFICULT

TO TAKE ON BY YOURSELF.

TAKE THIS TIME TO UTILIZE

THE PEOPLE AROUND YOU.

8.
PUTTING IT ALL TOGETHER

Your border is complete. Now it is time to fill in the pieces
that will bring the big picture to life.

Spread your wings!

This new found confidence will open the door to some
pretty spectacular outcomes.

Jot It Down

What are some of the inner pieces you need to complete your bigger picture?

_____

_____

_____

_____

_____

_____

_____

_____

_____

_____

_____

_____

_____

_____

_____

_____

_____

_____

_____

_____

_____

Go outside the security of your safety zone. Try to find a new comfort level with something that has seemed impossible most of your life. After all, it takes something unusual and imaginative to bring us to a point of interest.

Once you start taking some chances, you will come to a place where you get excited and overjoyed with all the possibilities of something new. The trick is to take it slow and not get overly anxious or frightened with the opportunity presented.

> It can be pretty intimidating when you are faced with that big decision of whether you should move forward or not. You start imagining the worst and immediately want to crawl back to where you feel comfortable. At that point, take a few days to think about it. Or as they say, "Sleep on it."

Take some time to let your ideas digest. Personally, I know the first day my mind starts racing and I can't make it through the night without grabbing my notebook and pen. But hold yourself back, take some time to let the ideas and emotions sink in.

If you're a person of strong faith, like myself, you may find praying on it to be very helpful.

Above all don't let the passion weigh you down mentally. The great thing about feeling passionate about something is that it is a natural emotion. **You will know whether you should act on it just by listening to what your mind, body, heart, and soul are telling you.** When all of those things are in sync, you will know it is right!

Be sure to look at all your options and consider the worst case scenario. If the worst thing that could happen is rejection, then what do you have to lose? It's your idea!! It's your thought!! That's what makes it amazing, exciting and exhilarating. Rejection is just someone else's opinion.

Put some deep thought into what you are doing. **What are the positive and negative of your decisions? Will it help other people? Will it hurt someone you love?** These are all important things to consider and could make a difference as to whether you continue on in the direction you are headed.

If anything that you do or say because of this choice is going to hurt anyone mentally or physically then you know you need to go a different direction. **Remember how it feels to be on the receiving end of negative words and actions.** You definitely don't want to be forwarding that on to someone else.

Jot It Down

How does it make you feel when someone starts throwing negative or derogatory words your way?

_____

_____

_____

_____

_____

_____

_____

_____

_____

_____

_____

_____

_____

_____

_____

_____

_____

_____

Go back and look at where you are in your life.

   • What have you achieved?

   • Did you reach your accomplishments because
   you were passionate or because someone told
   you it was the logical thing to do?

   • Has most of it been a result of what you truly
   felt zealous about or was it the circumstances
   life threw at you along the way?

Put some serious thought into it. It will make a big
difference in your perspective and you will be amazed,
when you back up and peek at your past, what your true
answers really are.

Jot It Down

List some of your accomplishments and the people who
encouraged you.

_____

_____

_____

_____

_____

_____

_____

_____

_____

_____

_____

_____

_____

_____

_____

_____

_____

_____

The main thing is to move forward. Don't look back. If you feel it in your gut and you know it is the right thing to do, then do it! Press on! Make the changes in your life that result in a better you.

Remember, **Rome wasn't built in a day and the Titanic had a deadline.** Everything good starts with something small and over time turns into something magnificent!

Don't worry if there is no one else that agrees with what you are trying to do. Put everything you have into it and have no regrets.

When you have achieved your aspiration, the overwhelming feeling of accomplishment is worth the agony you might have gone through to get there. Accomplishment is something that will stay with you forever.

Ask yourself the appropriate questions. Keep in mind that you are trying to make a difference in your life which eventually will make a difference in someone else's.

If you have a decision to make and the outcome means that someone is going to be hurt by your actions, you know it is not an idea worth pursuing. Think about how your words or actions will affect the people around you. Be a person that is proud of their achievements and triumphs.

Write down words of encouragement and tape them to your mirror. Post them to your refrigerator and anywhere else you know you will be visiting on a daily basis. Make a point to look at them consistently every day!

Jot It Down

List some positive affirmations that you can use to keep you inspired and motivated.

There will always be roadblocks — both mental and physical. It's a part of life. They are not there to stop you but to make you stronger.

The old adage is true: **"What doesn't kill you, makes you stronger."** Roadblocks give you something to think about and sometimes force you to get off the fence. You will be amazed at how far you get once you put your mind to it.

Jot It Down

What could possibly be some of your roadblocks preventing you from being yourself?

_____

_____

_____

_____

_____

_____

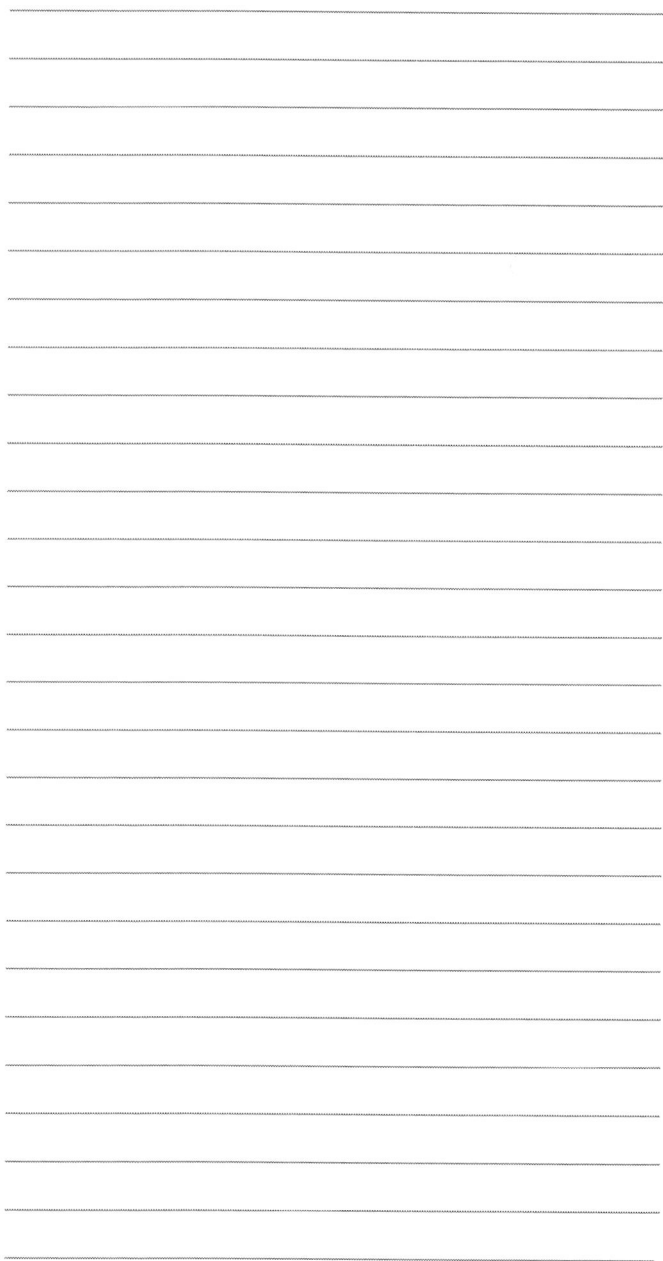

When you feel deeply about something, it doesn't go away. It will always be there in the back of your mind, constantly nagging at you to grab it. Make it yours! It was given to you for a reason. Don't let it slip away.

Keep on keepin' on!!!

The road may be long or it may be just a short jaunt. Whatever it is, you are going to make it memorable. There are no regrets, because no matter how it turns out, it's yours! It's something you accomplished that you felt passionate about. **Be proud of where you are and what you have done!**

Words of Encouragement

There is good in each of us!

It is our circumstances in life
that misguide us.

Believe that you were meant
to do amazing and incredible things.

Record it on a recorder,
tape it to your mirror.

Whatever you have to do,
don't ever give up!

I have complete confidence
that you will accomplish
all you are capable of.

· · · *Exercises* · · ·

❶ Use the space below to list emotions, actions, people, places, things, etc. of the "old you" and the "new you."

Old You

_____

_____

_____

_____

_____

_____

_____

_____

_____

_____

_____

_____

_____

_____

_____

_____

_____

New You

❷ What are some things that, at one time seemed impossible for you to accomplish?

_____

_____

_____

_____

_____

_____

_____

_____

_____

_____

_____

_____

_____

_____

_____

_____

_____

_____

_____

_____

_____

_____

_____

❸ Looking at the items listed in Exercise 2, how do you feel now?

_____

_____

_____

_____

_____

_____

_____

_____

_____

_____

_____

_____

_____

_____

_____

_____

_____

_____

_____

_____

_____

_____

_____

❹ What are some of the first steps you will take to rediscovering the new you?

Positive Reminder

WHEN YOU HAVE ACHIEVED YOUR ASPIRATION,

THE OVERWHELMING FEELING

OF ACCOMPLISHMENT

IS WORTH THE AGONY YOU MIGHT

HAVE GONE THROUGH TO GET THERE.

GOOD LUCK AND GOD BLESS!

YOUR JOURNEY

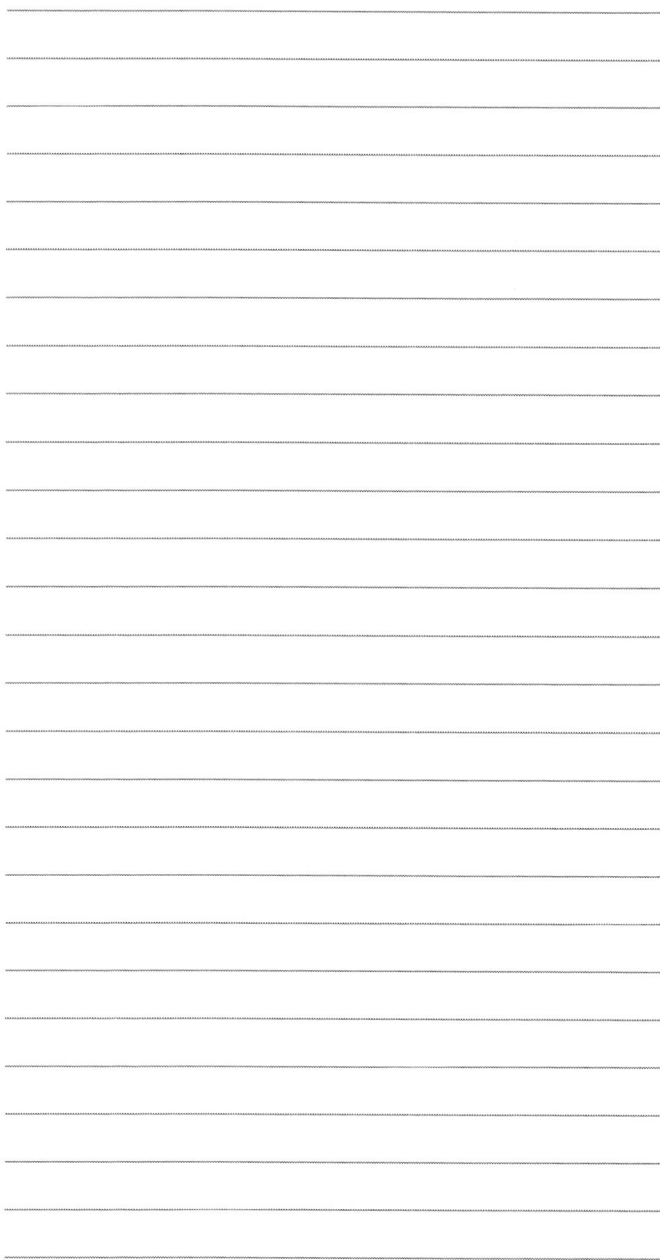